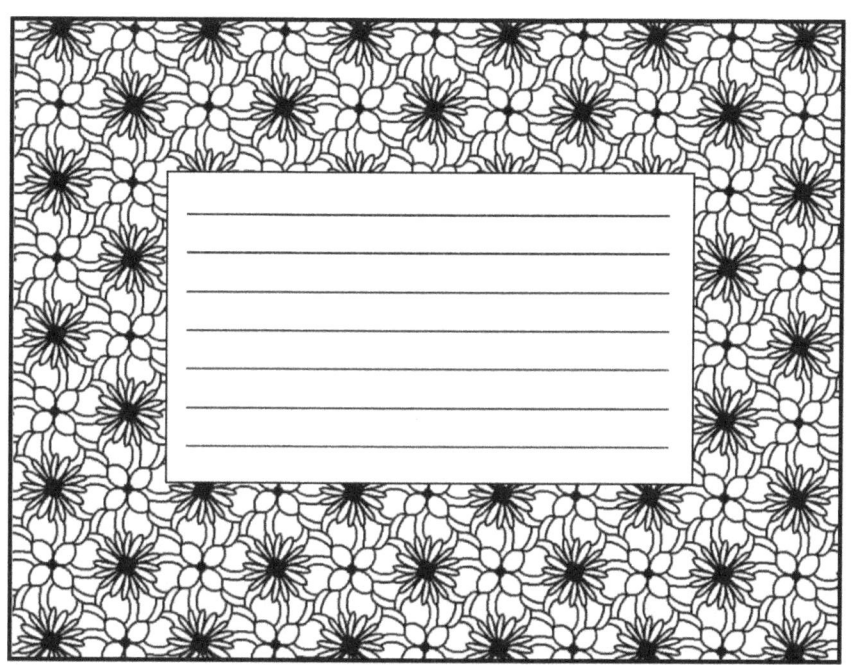

Test Page

Welcome to your test page! This is a great place to try out your favorite coloring materials and become familiar with the book's paper weight and thickness. You can use it to practice new coloring techniques too!

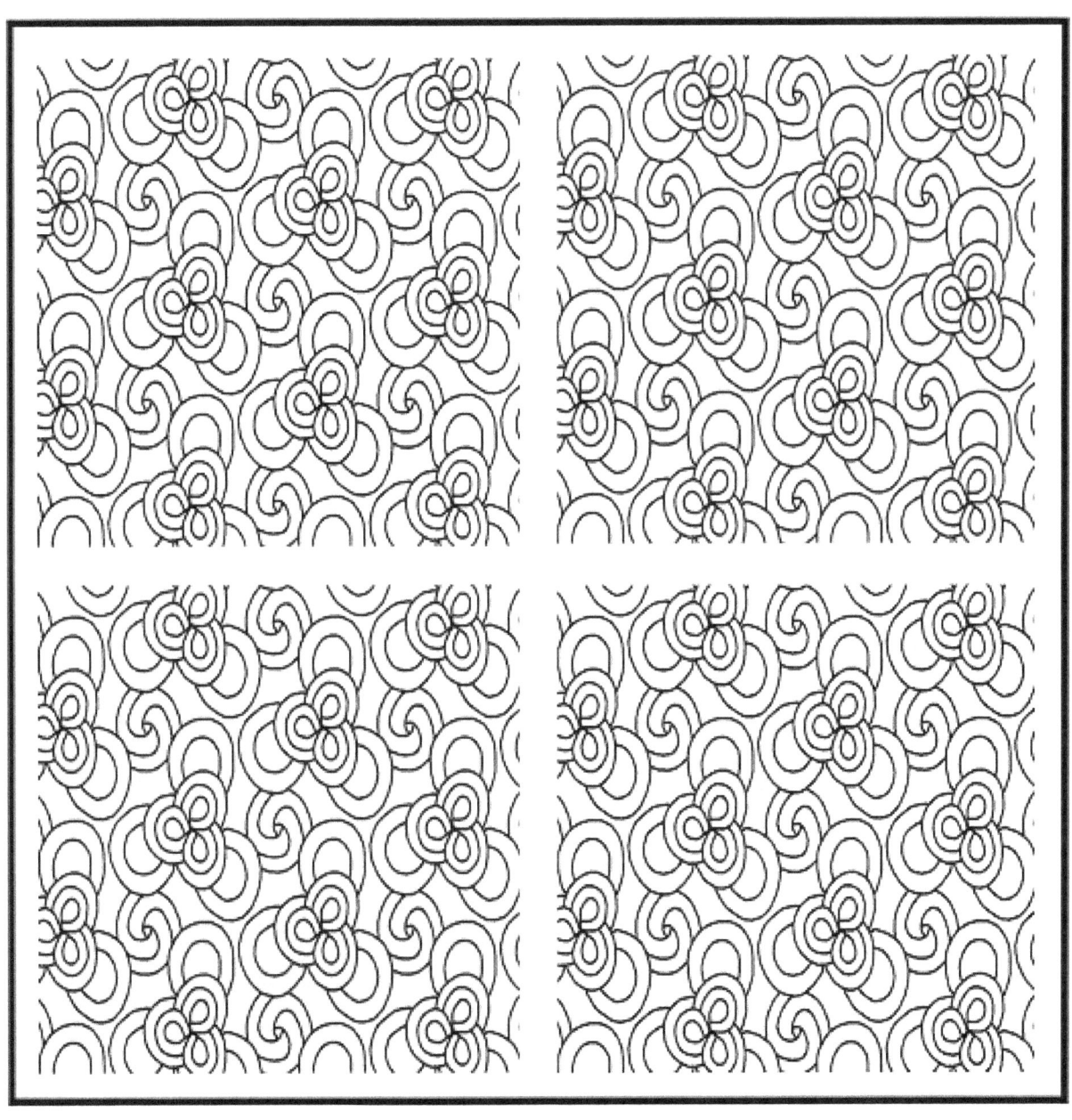

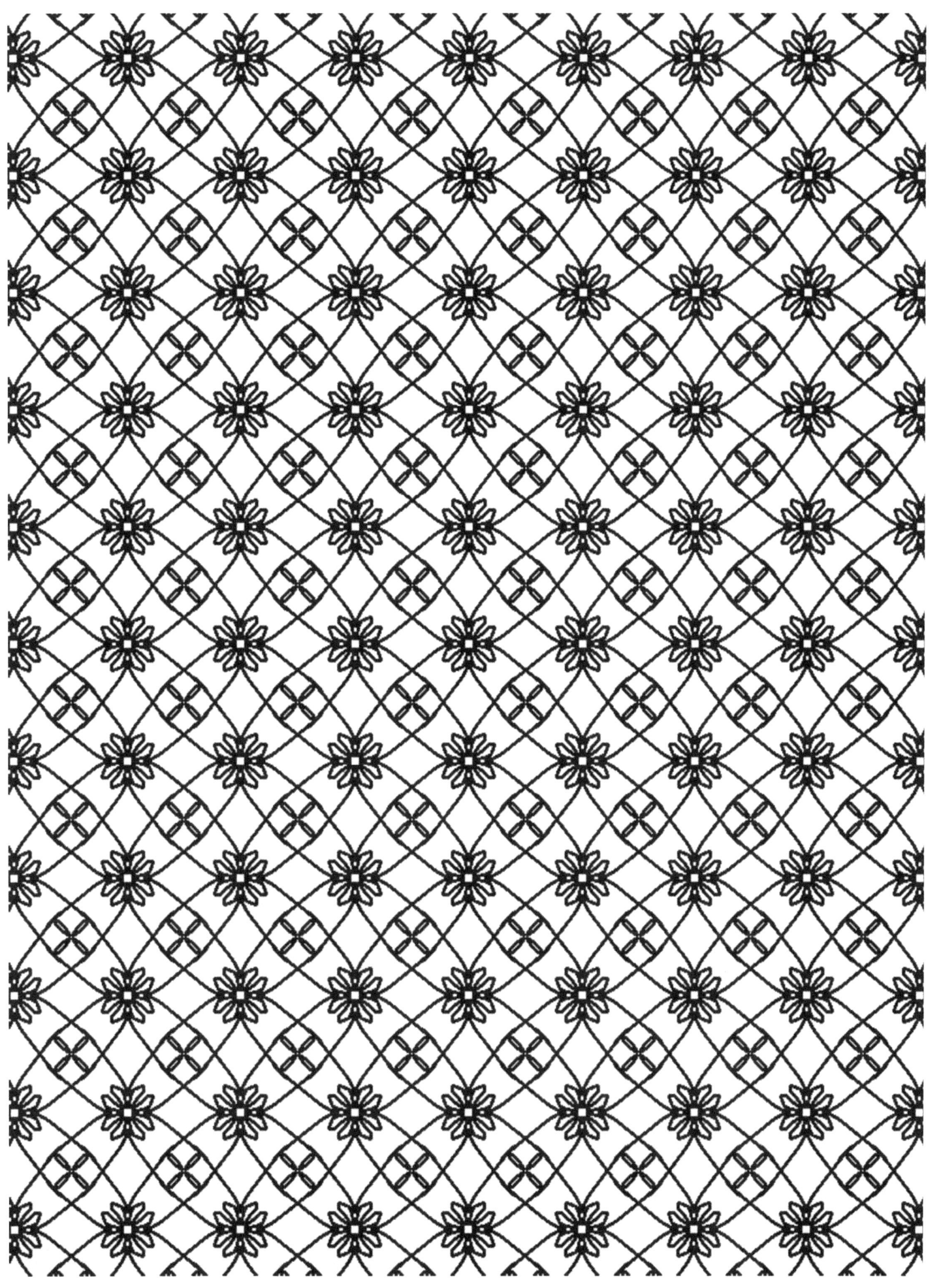

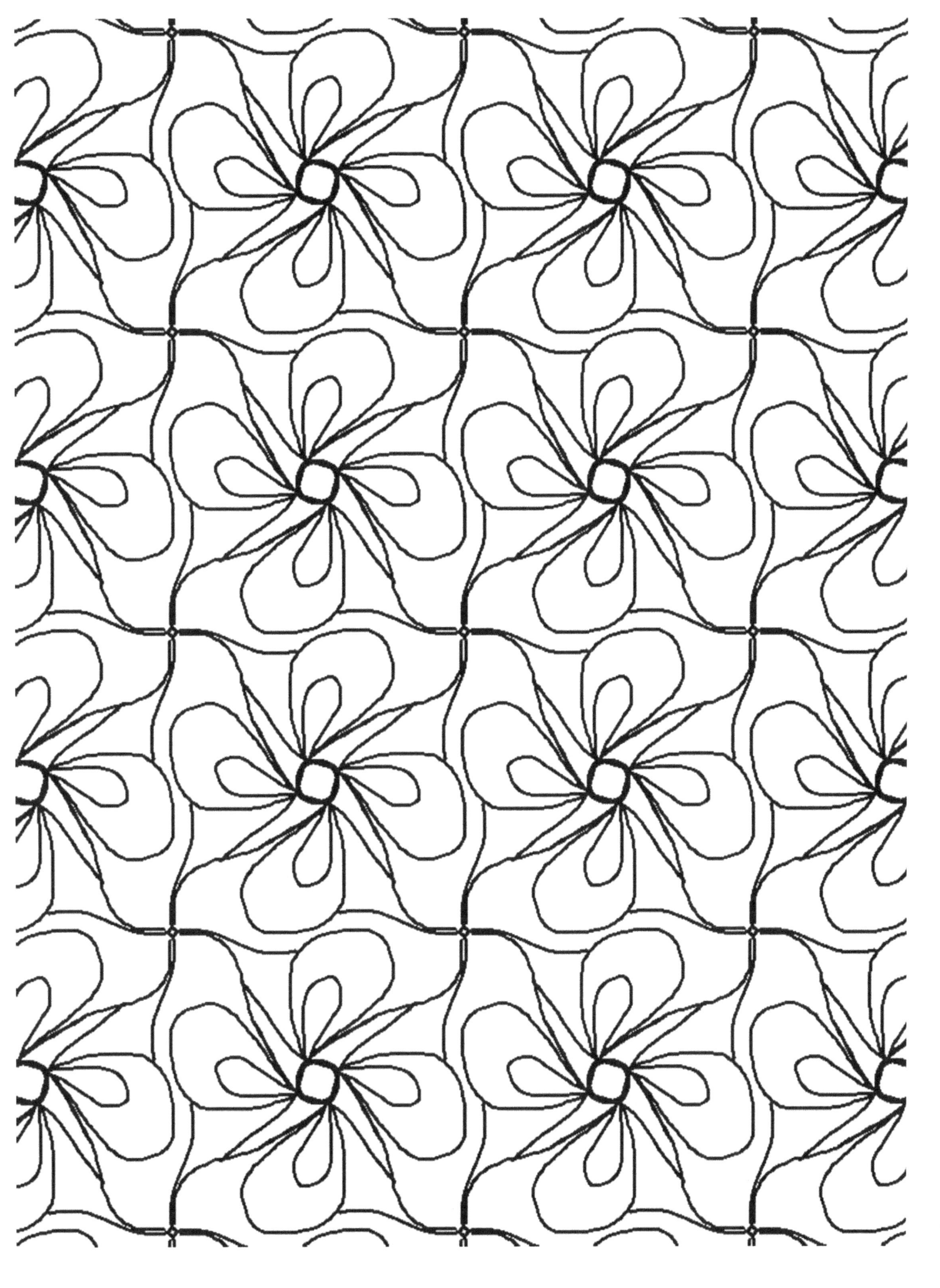

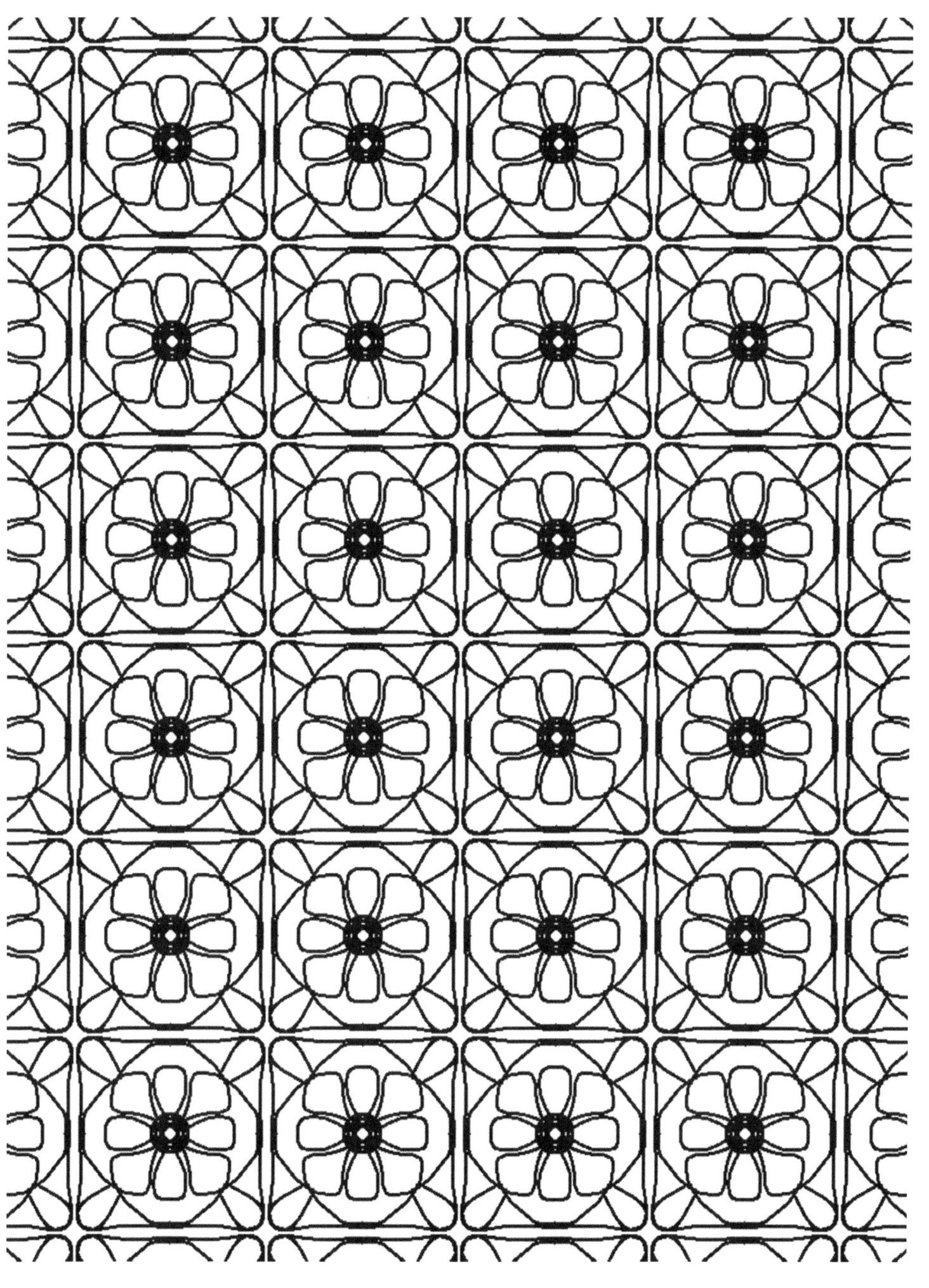

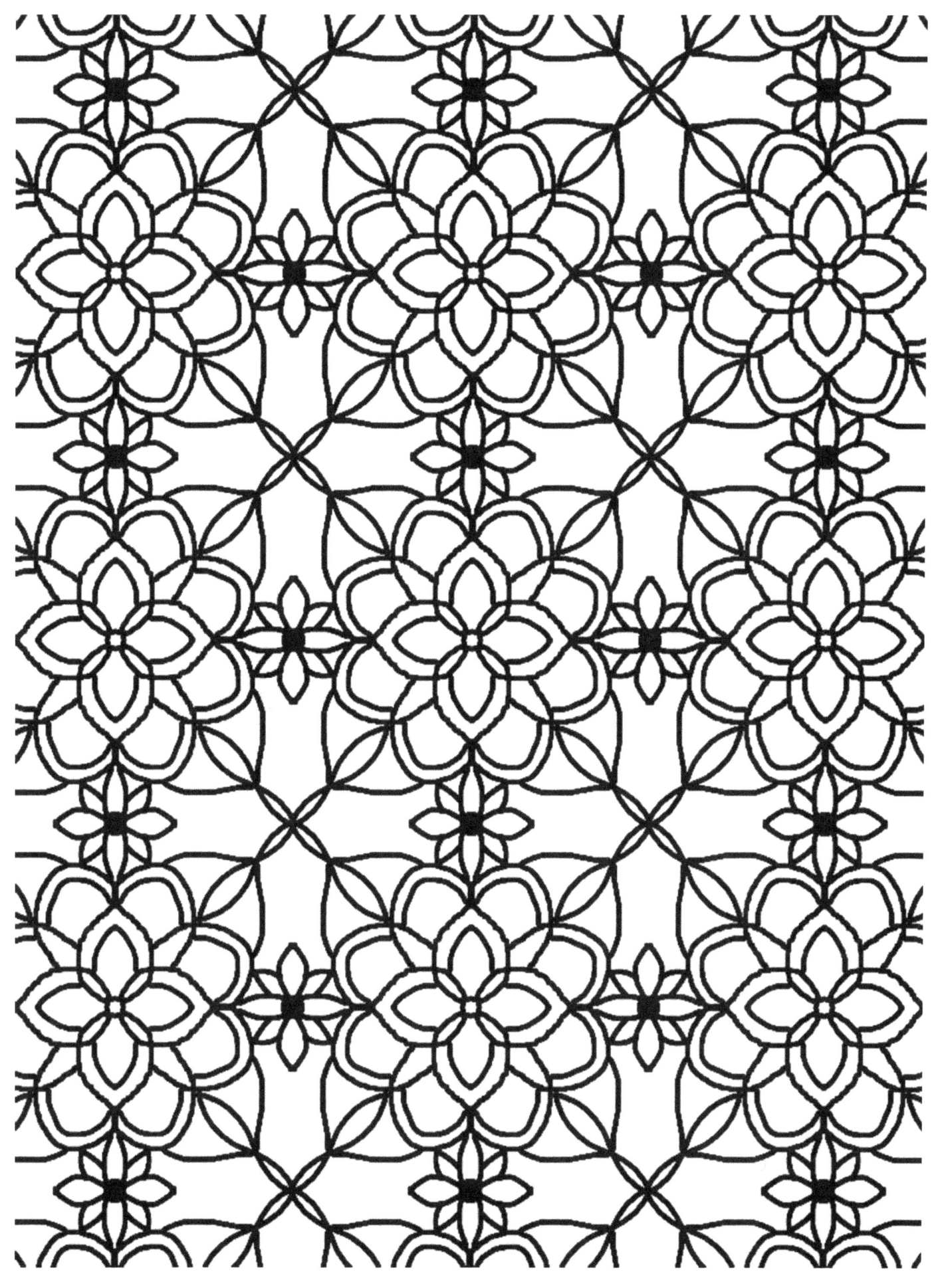

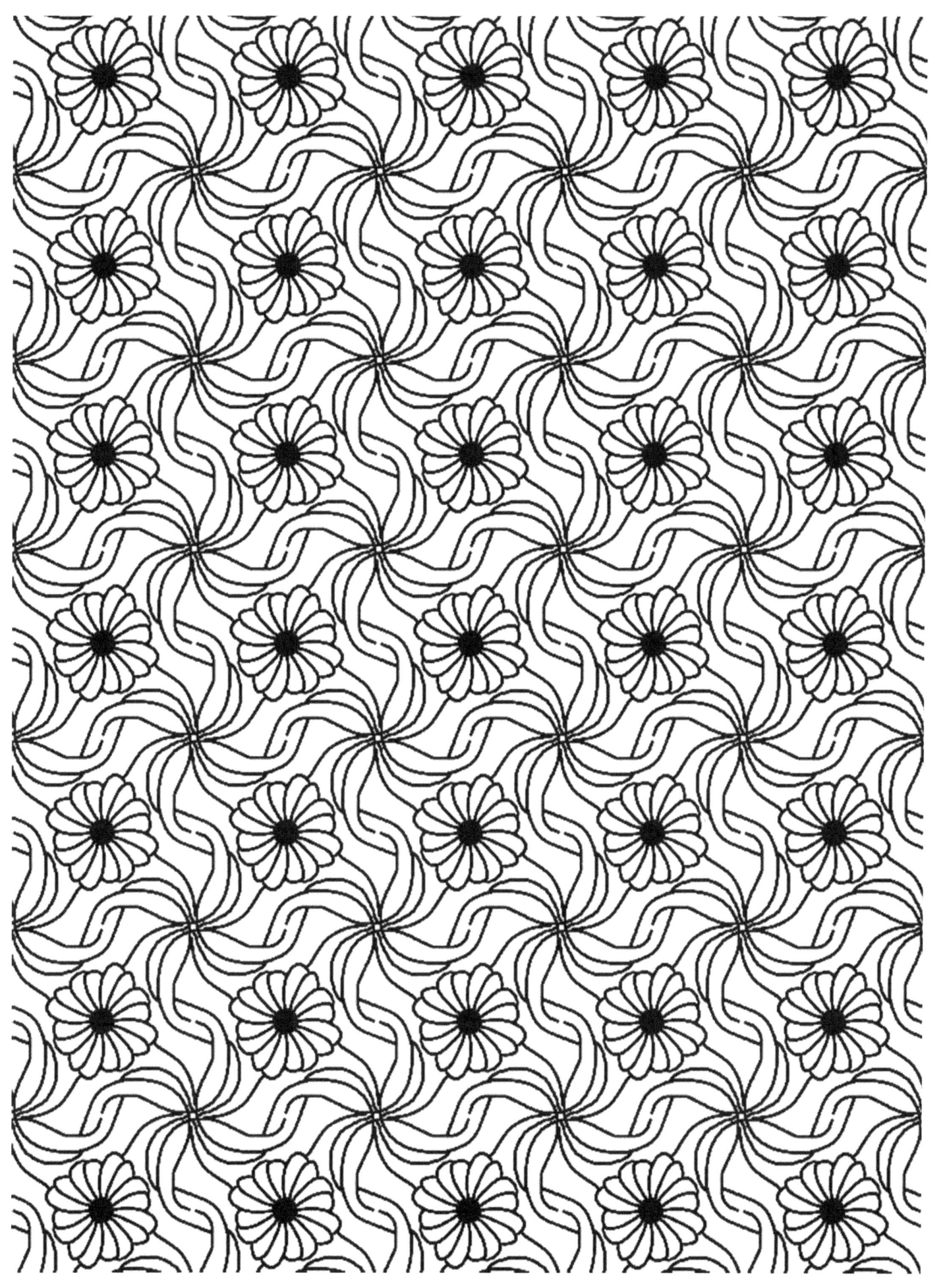

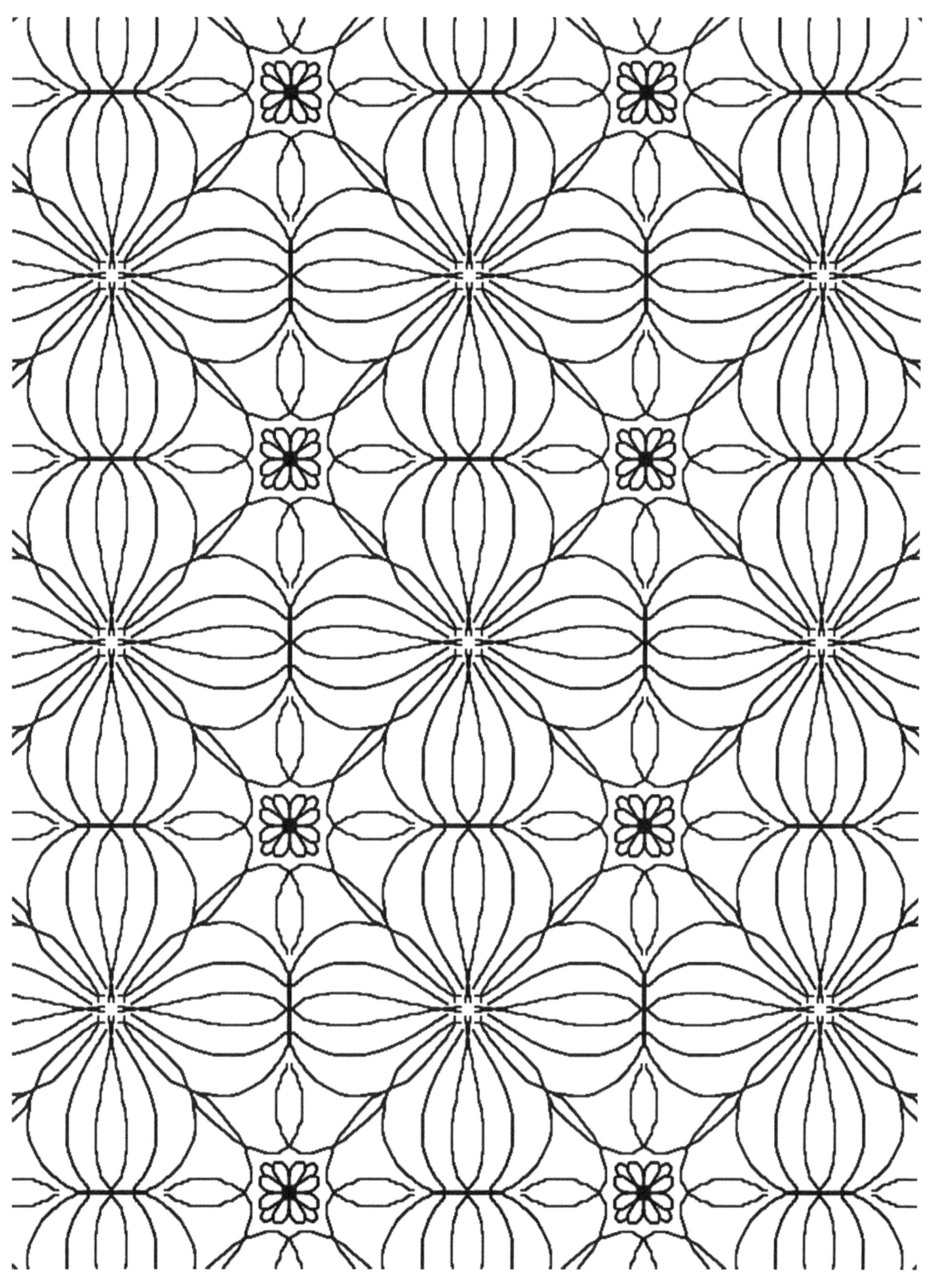

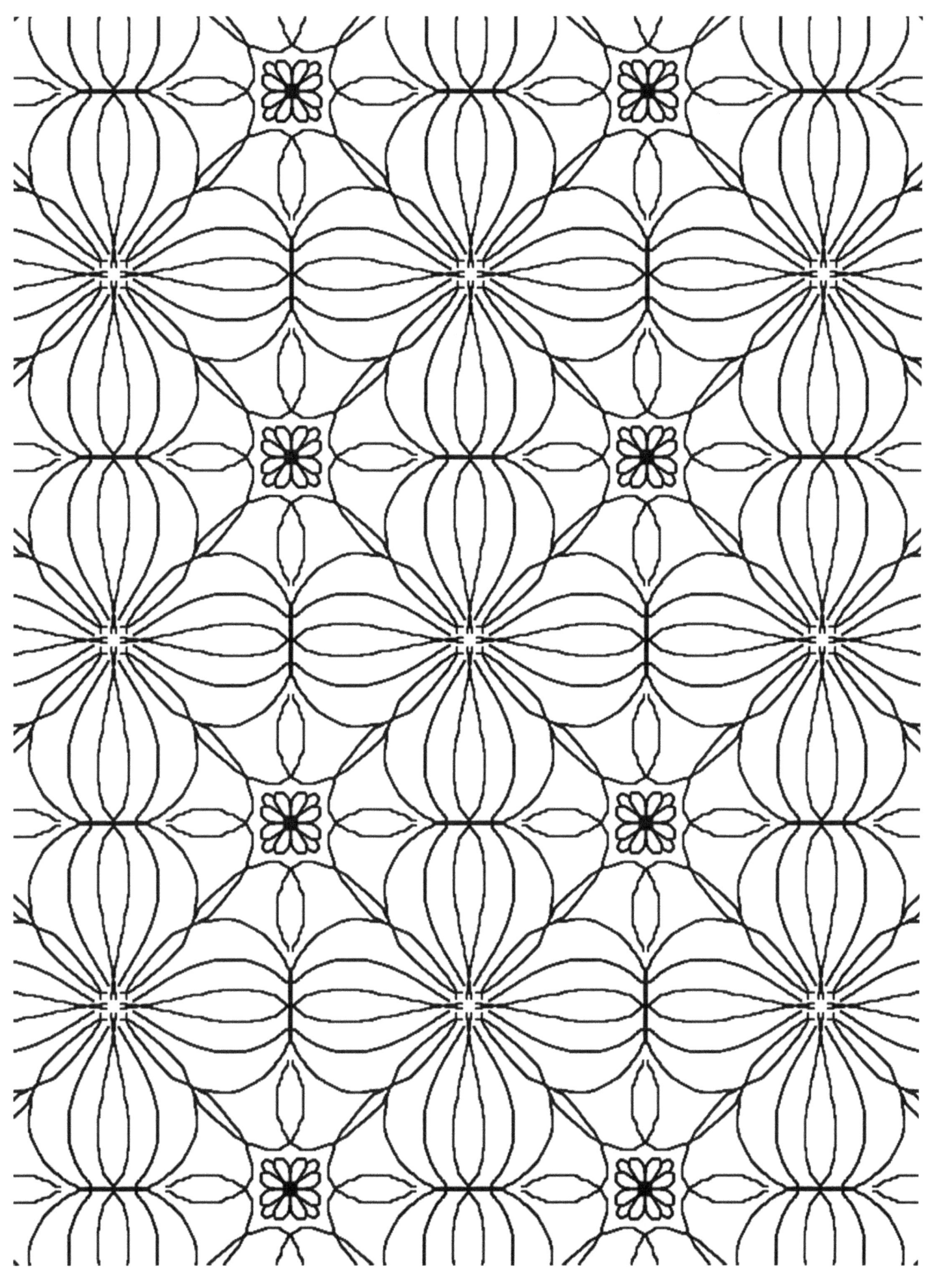

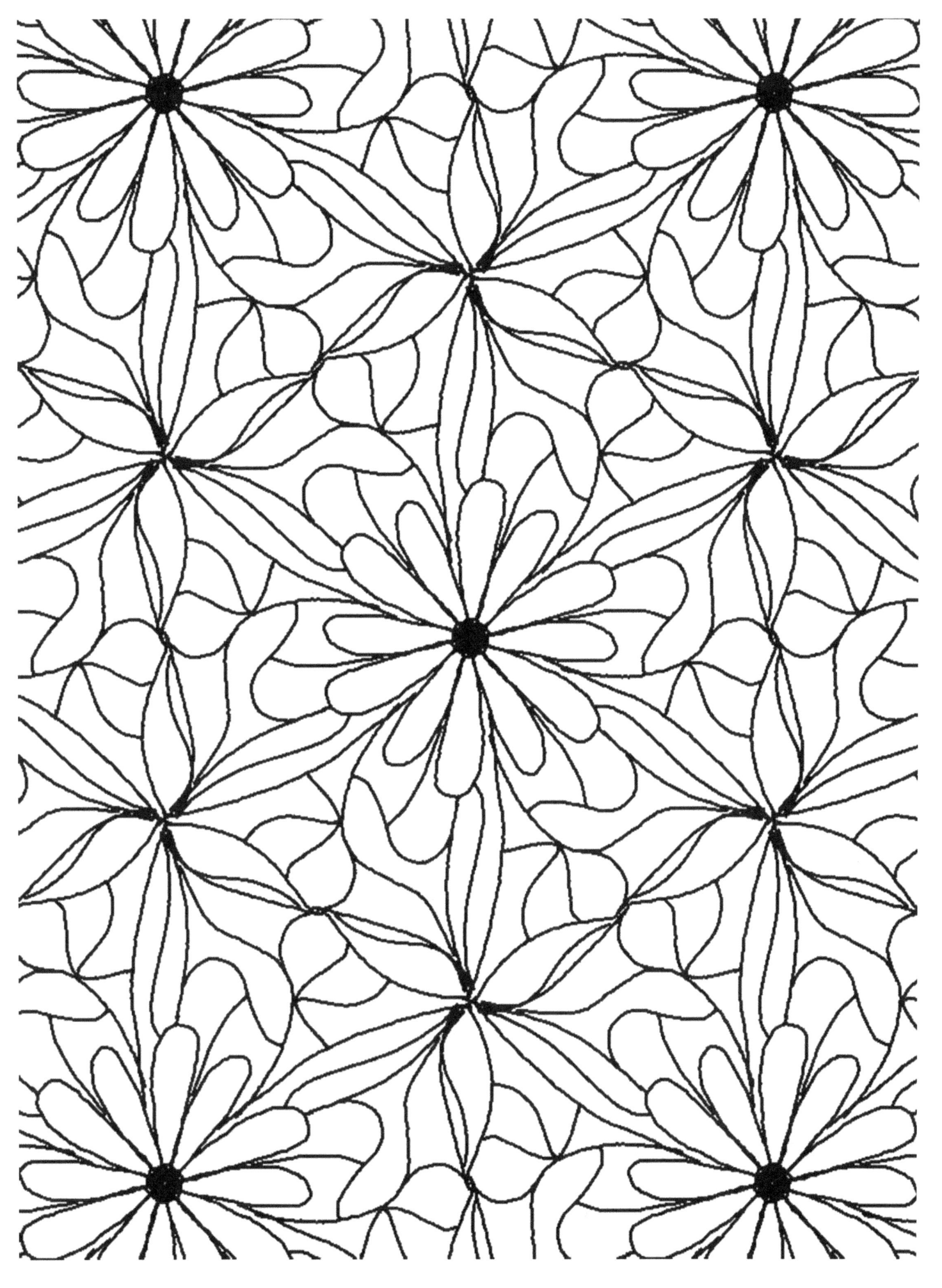

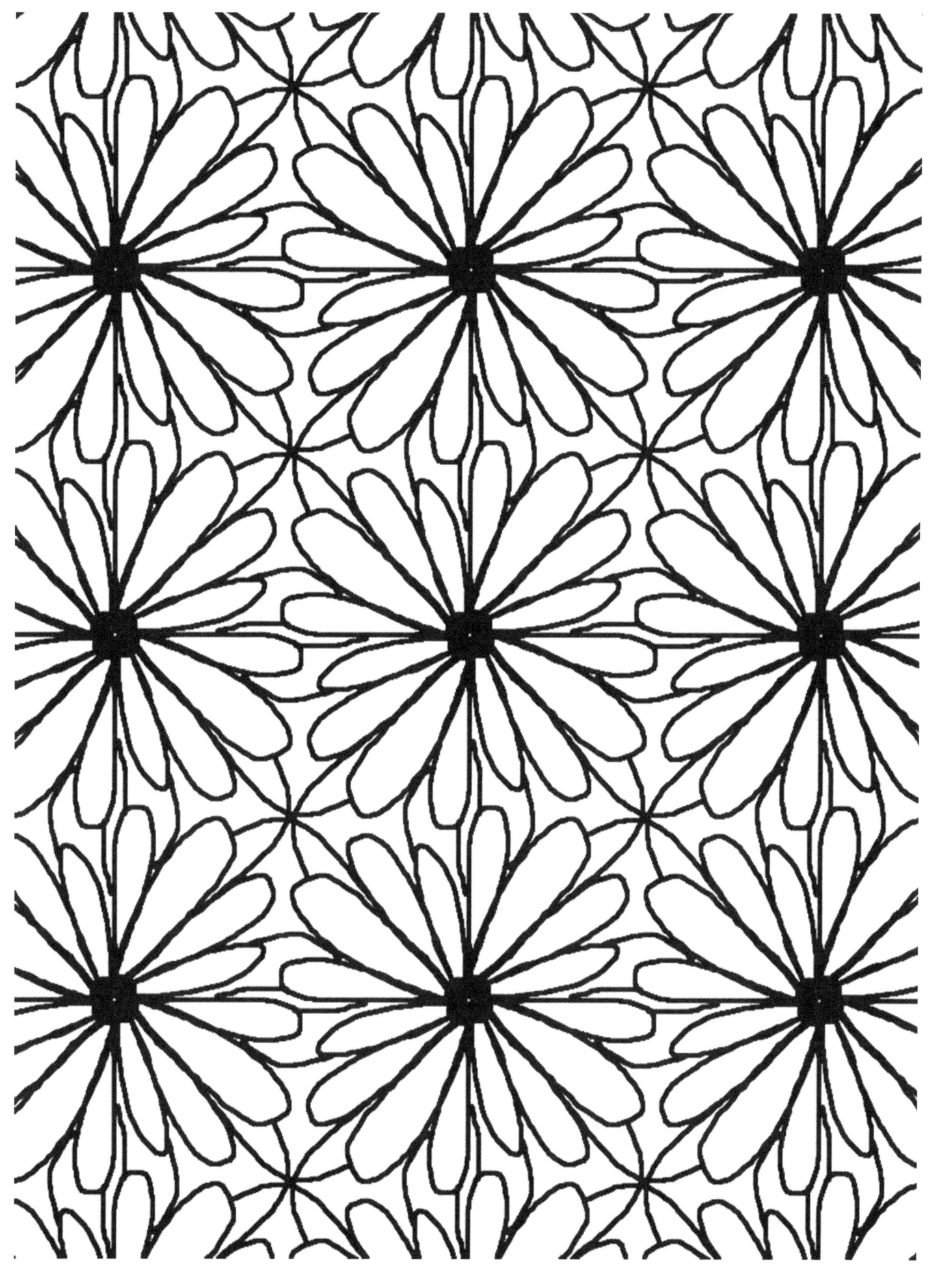

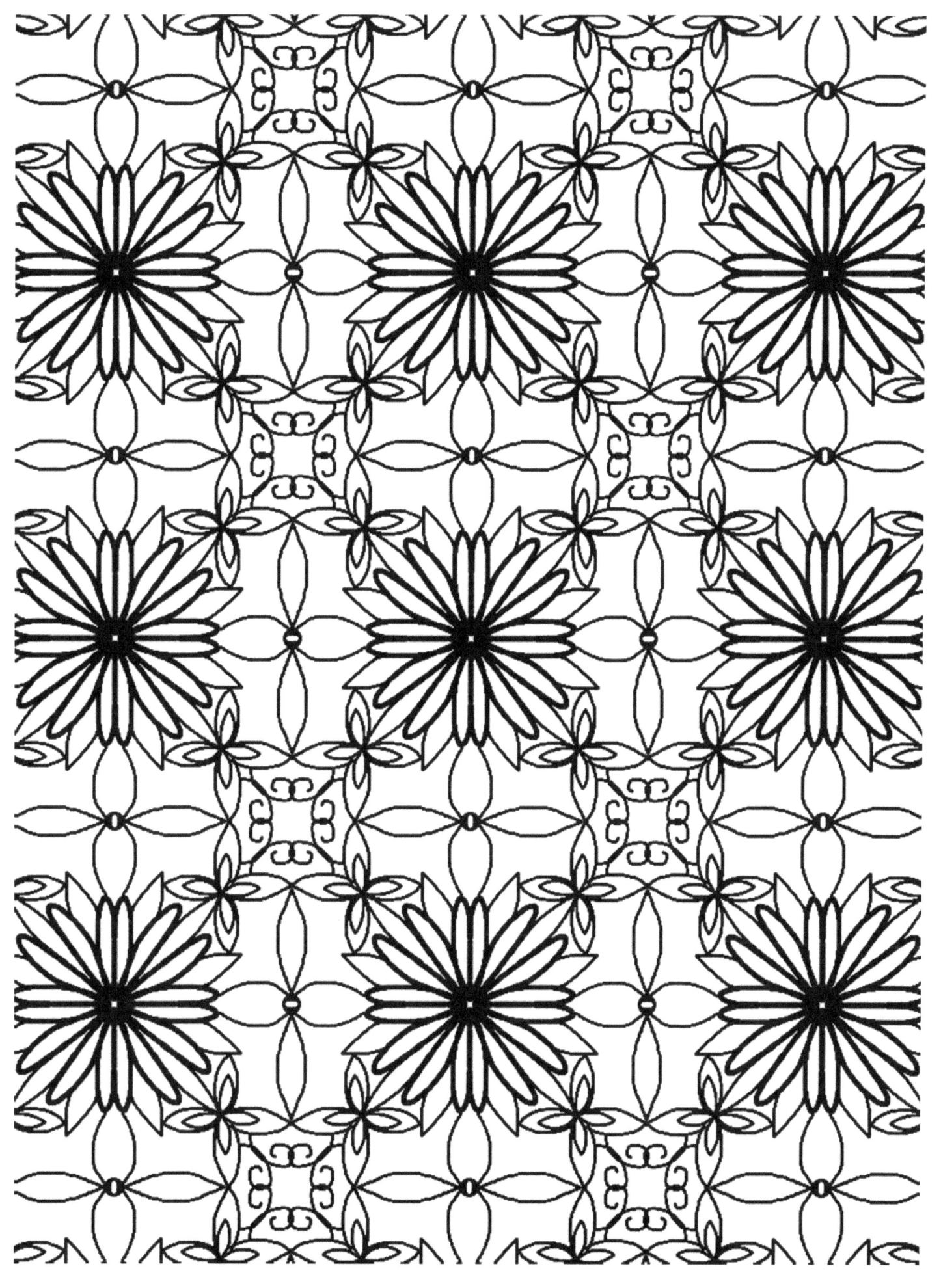

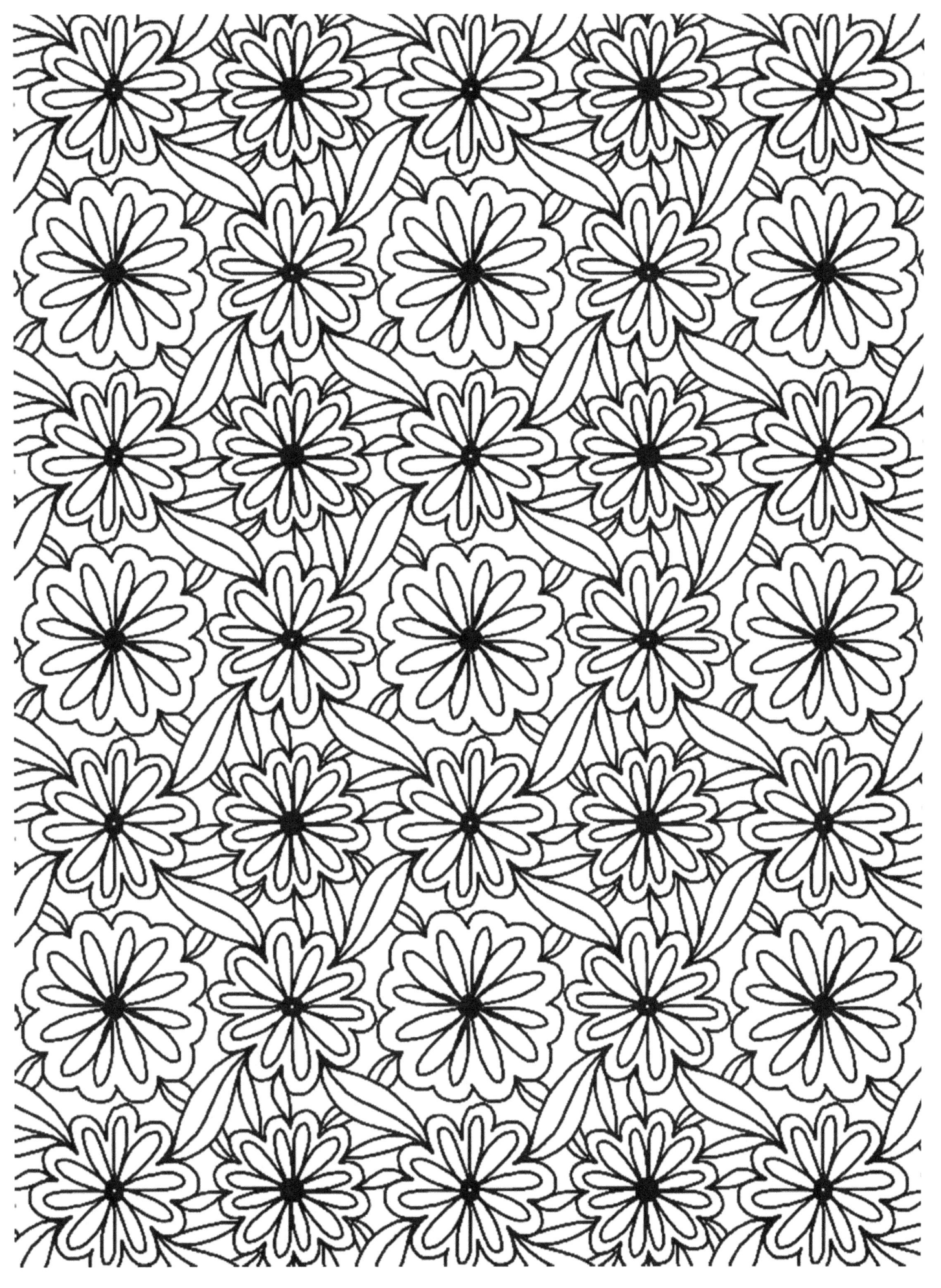

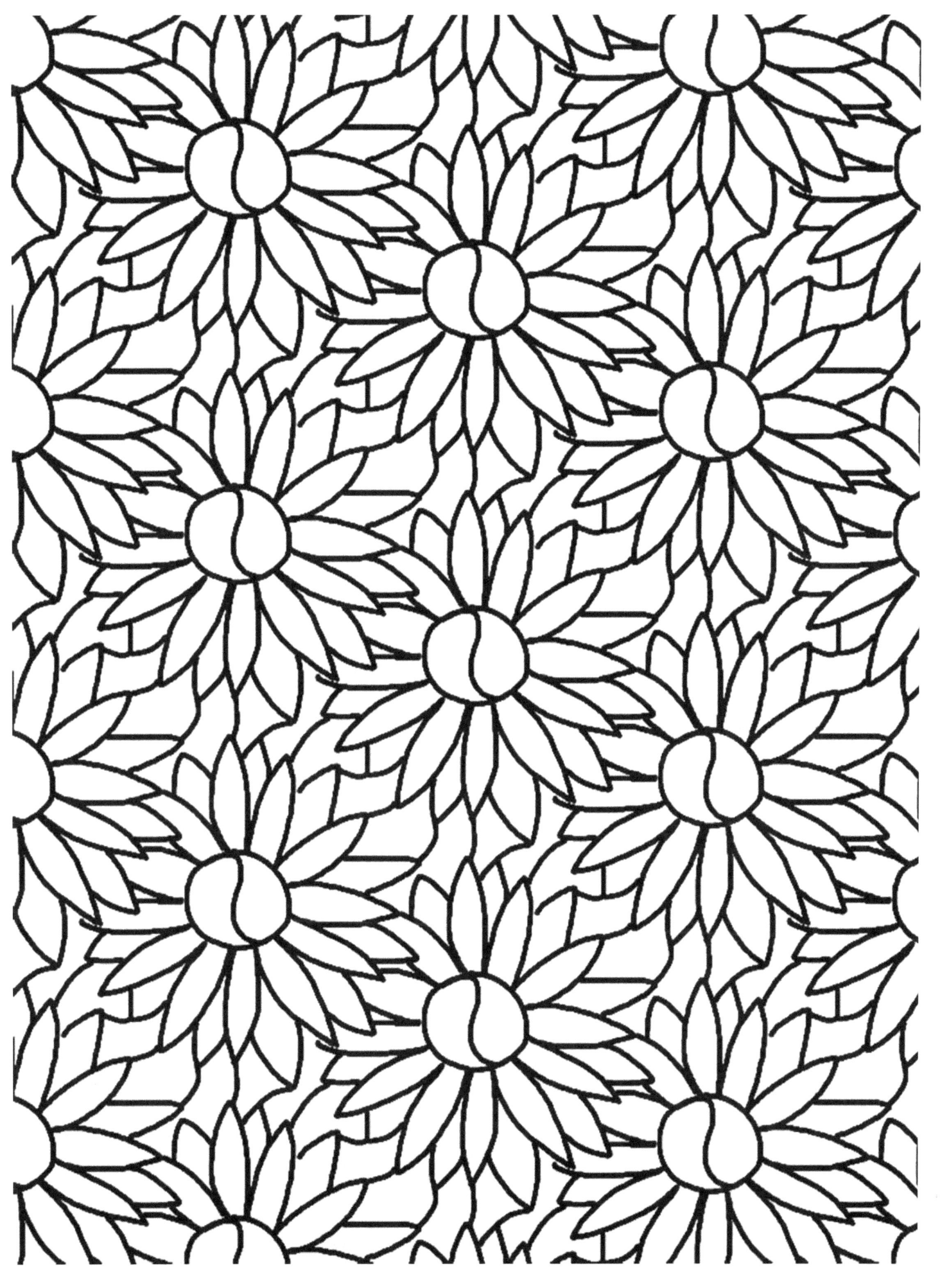

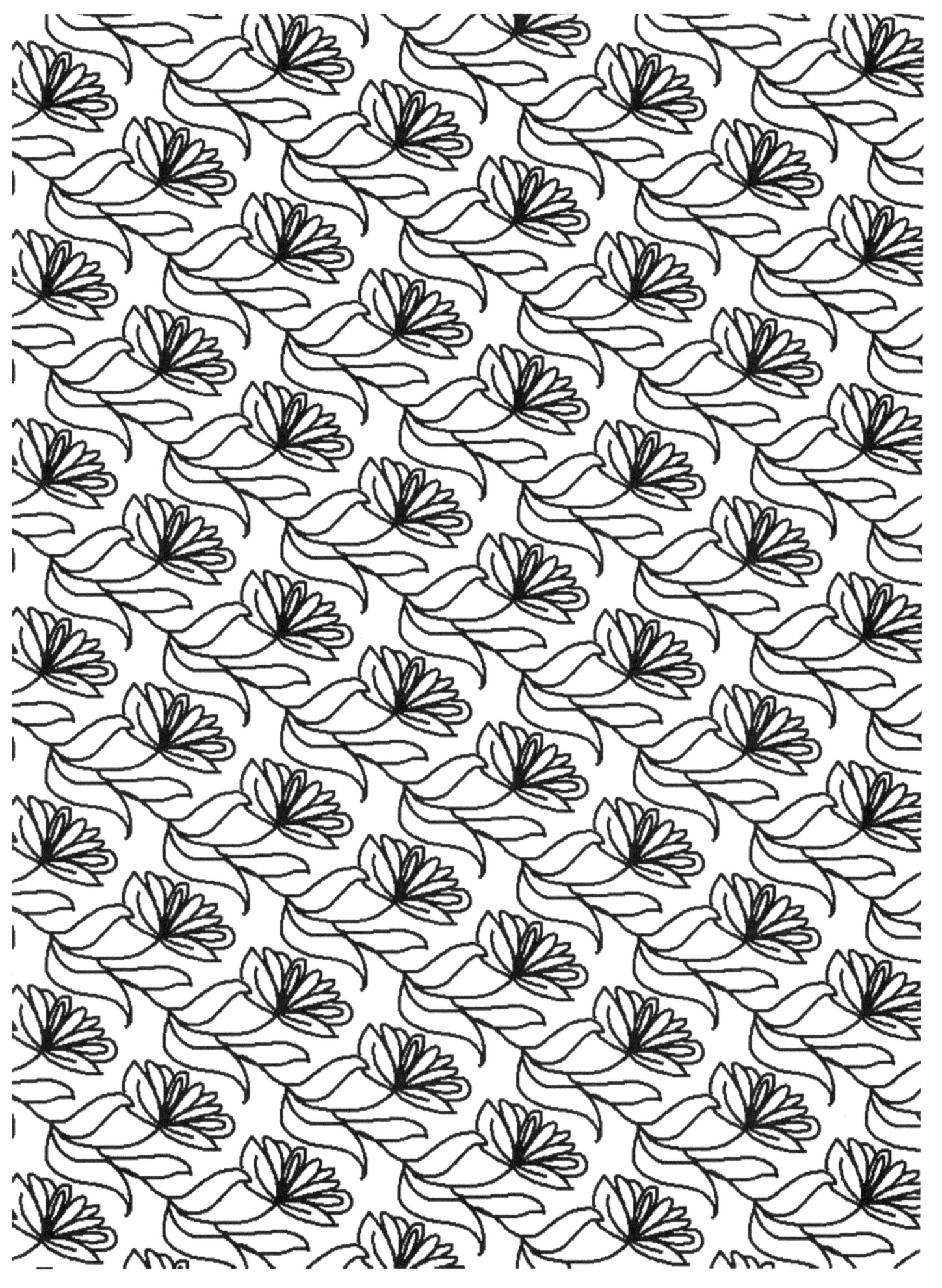

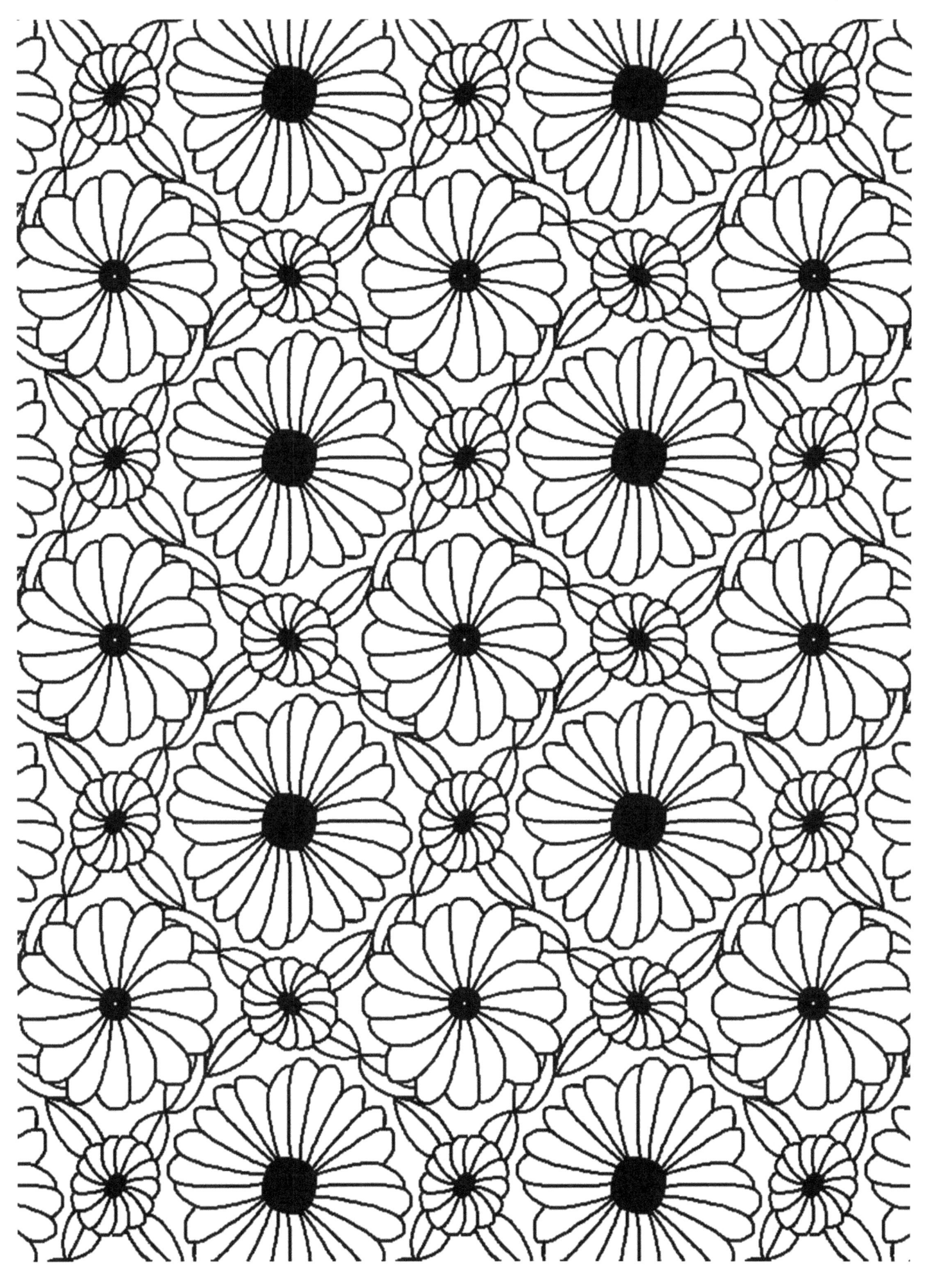

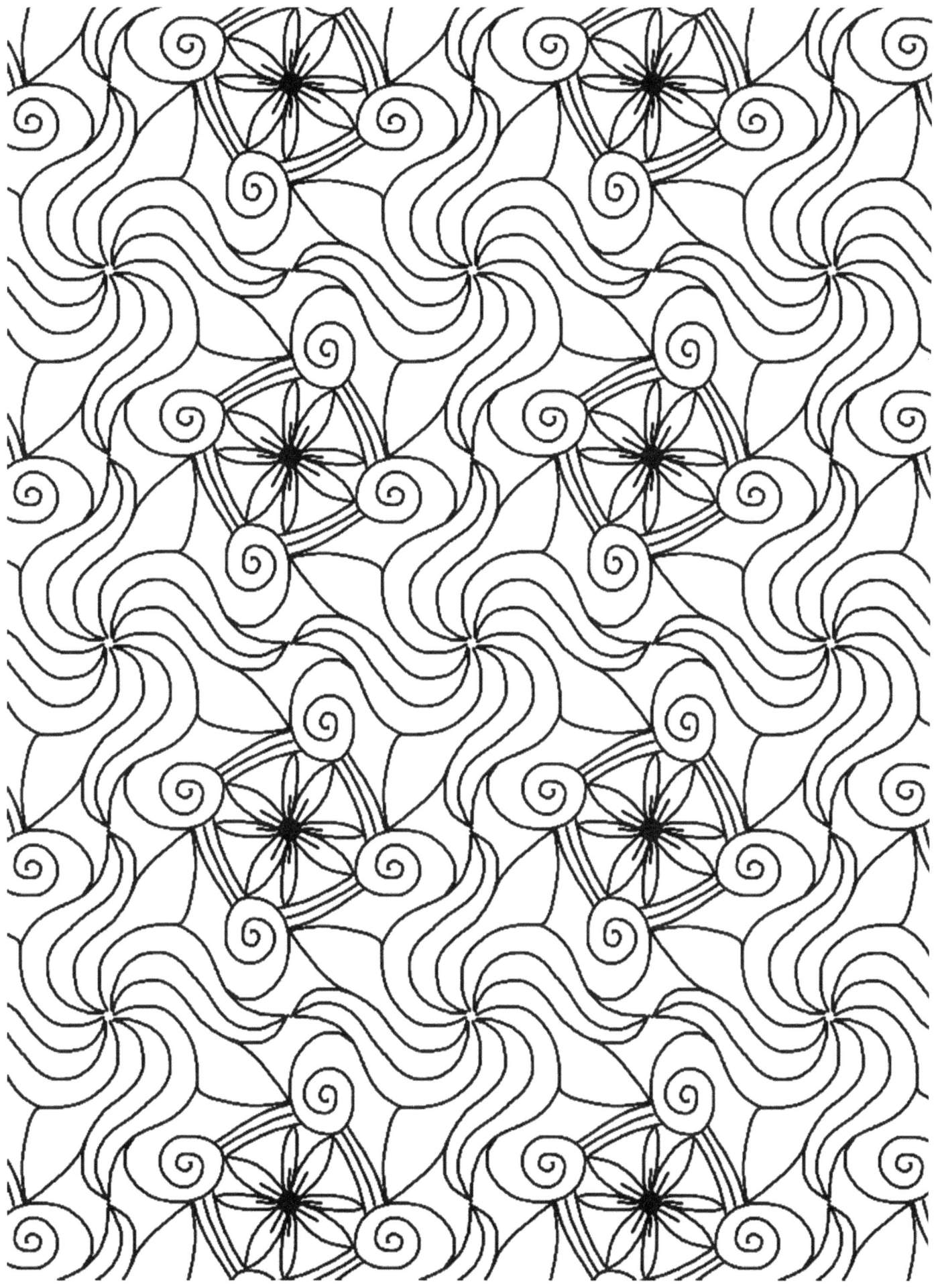

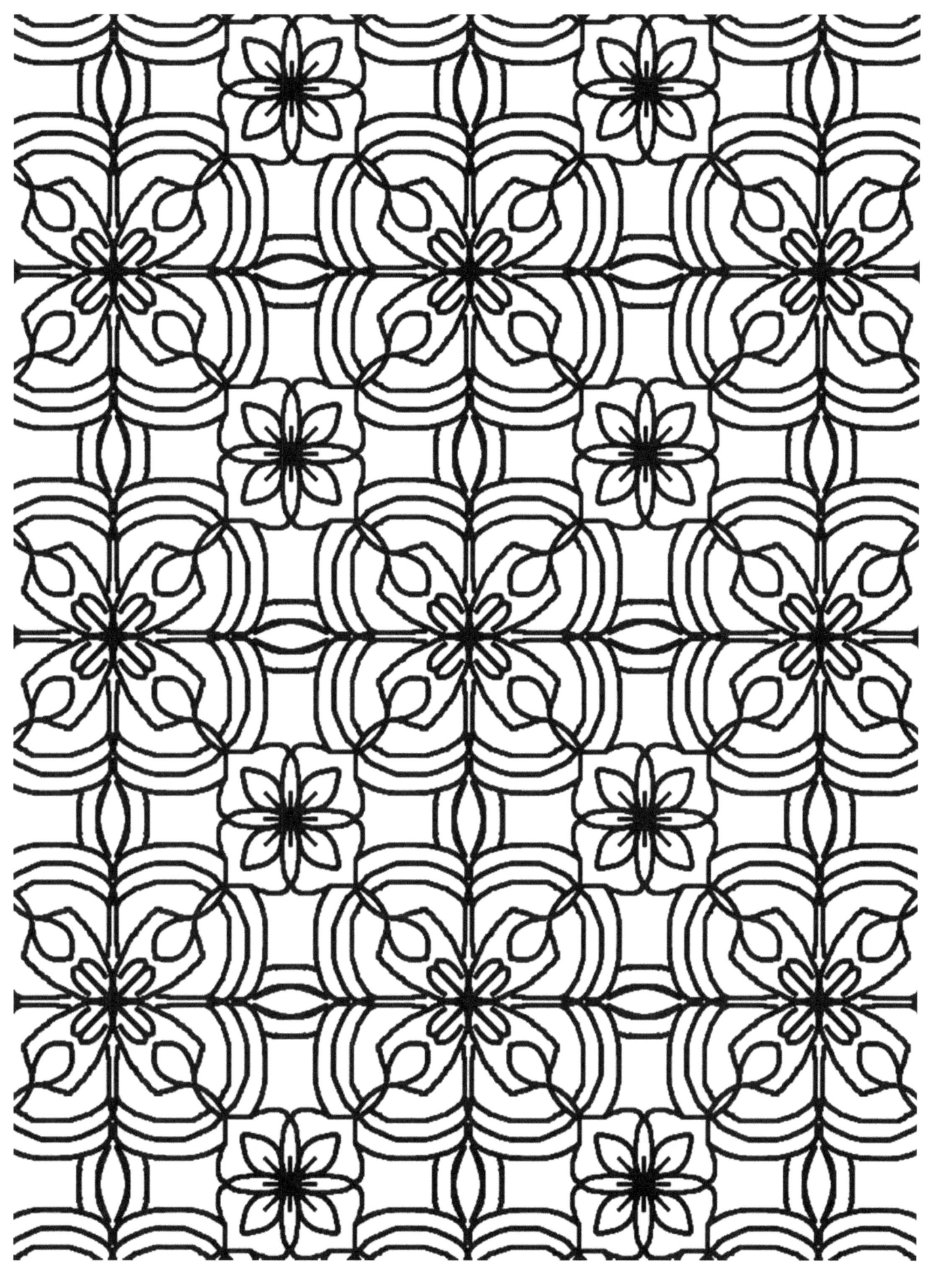

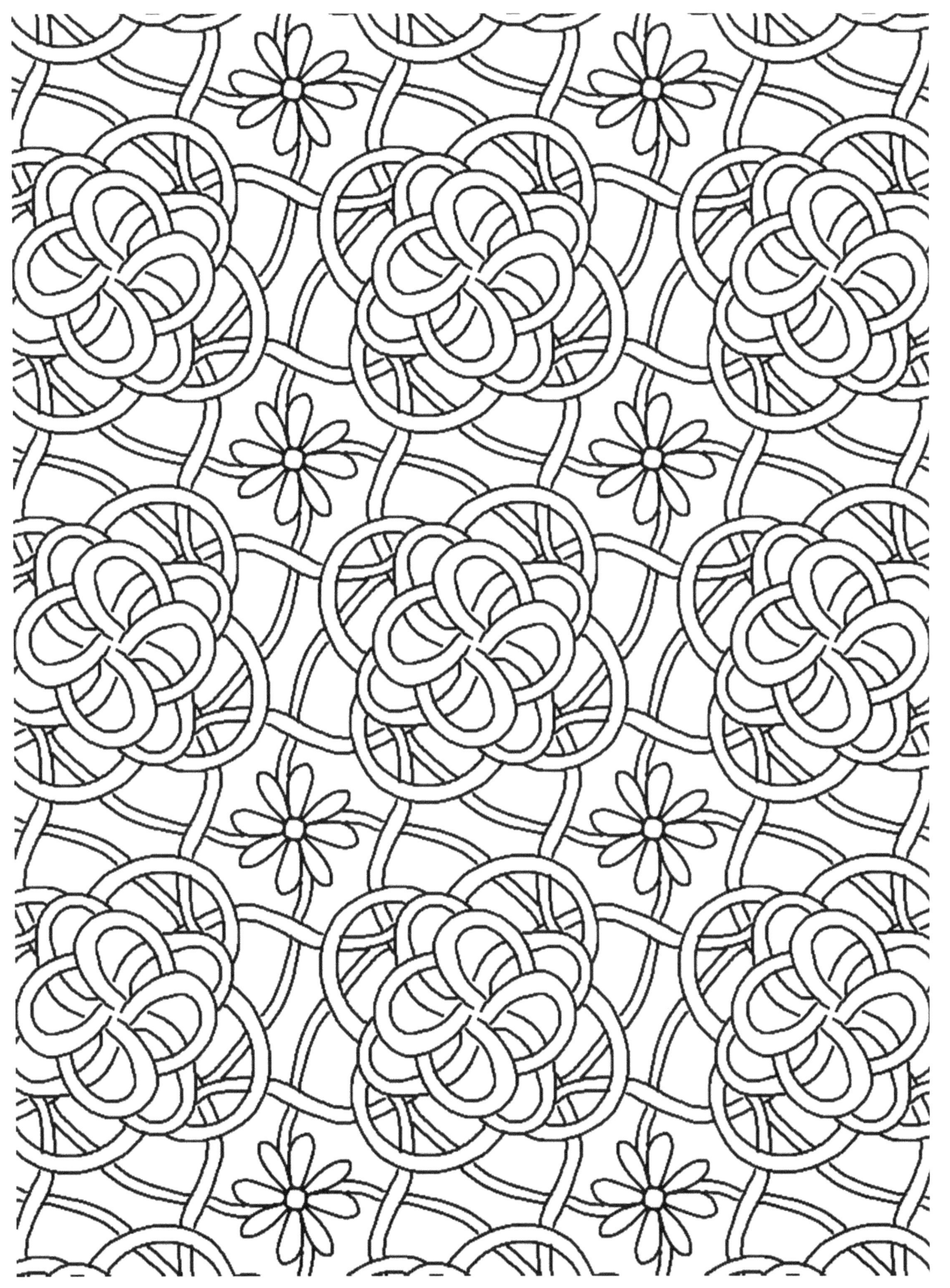

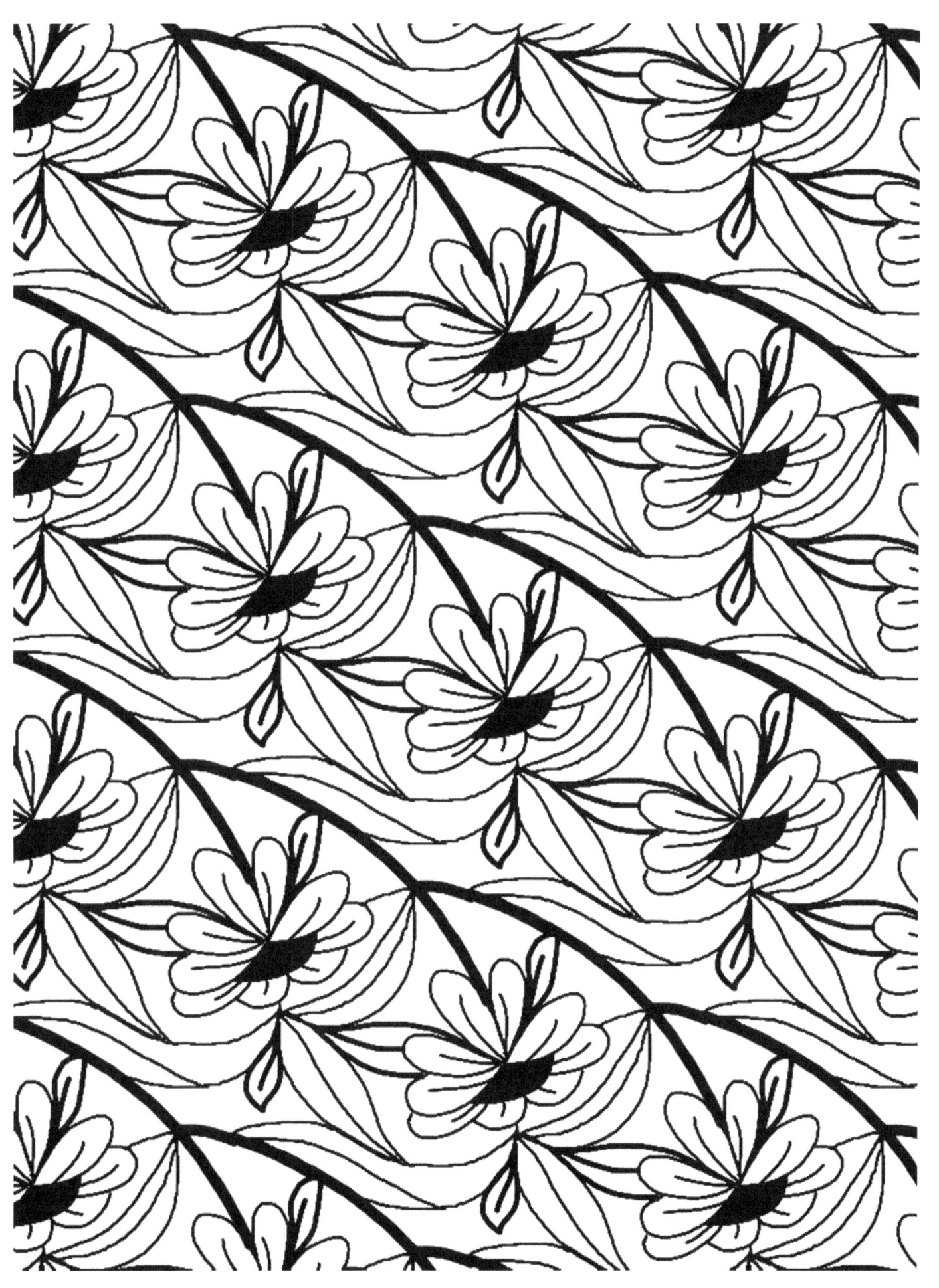

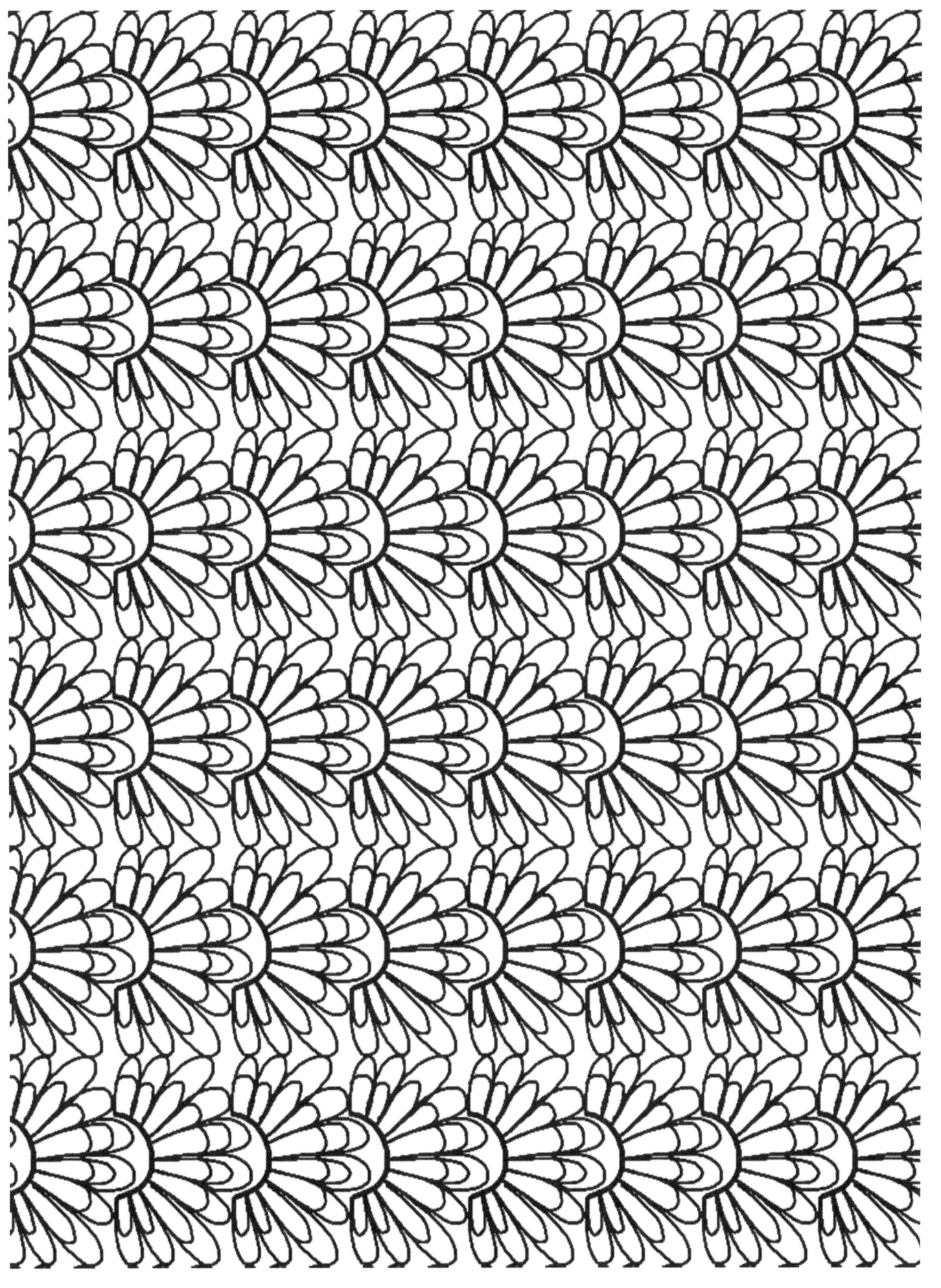

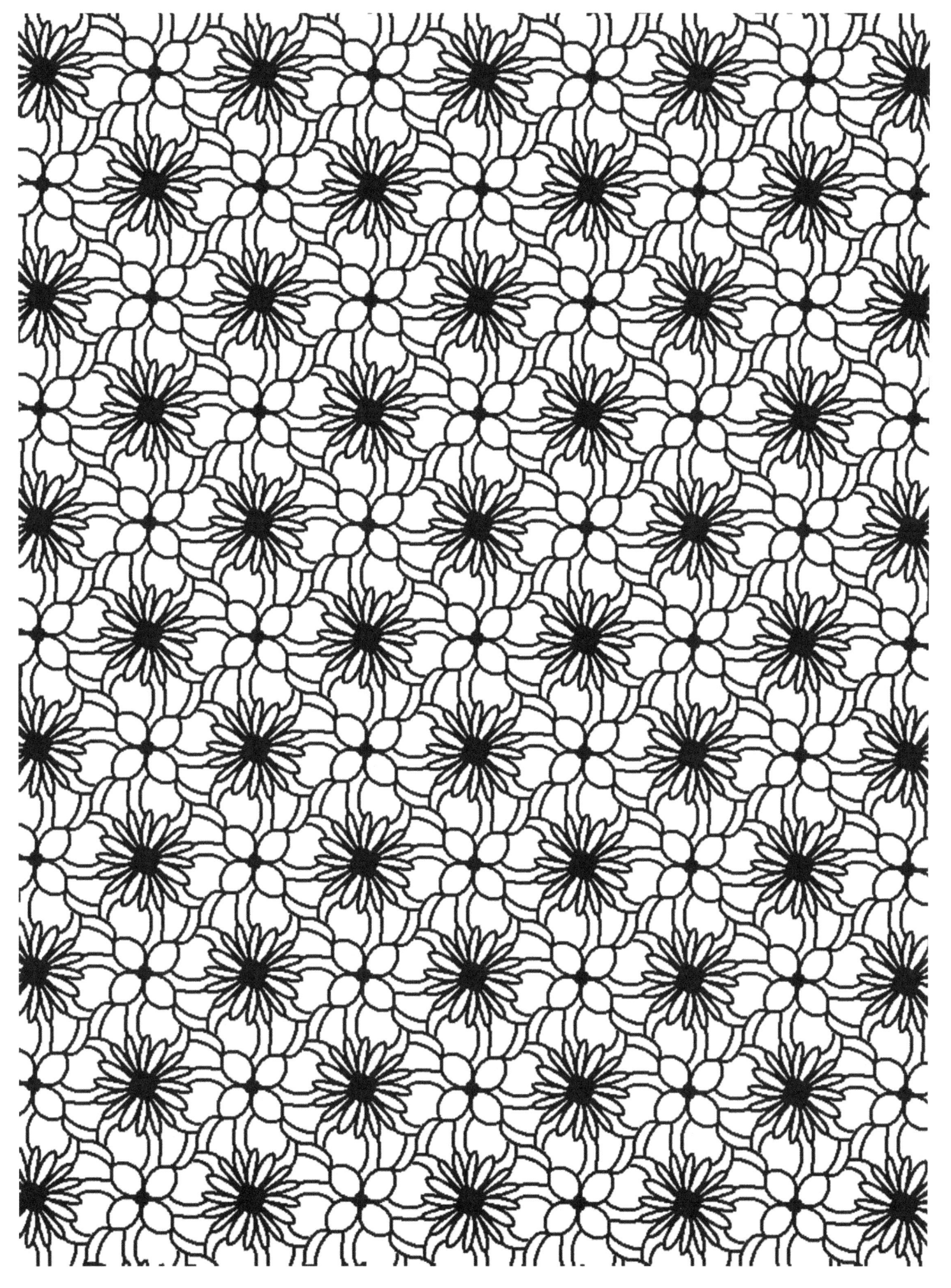

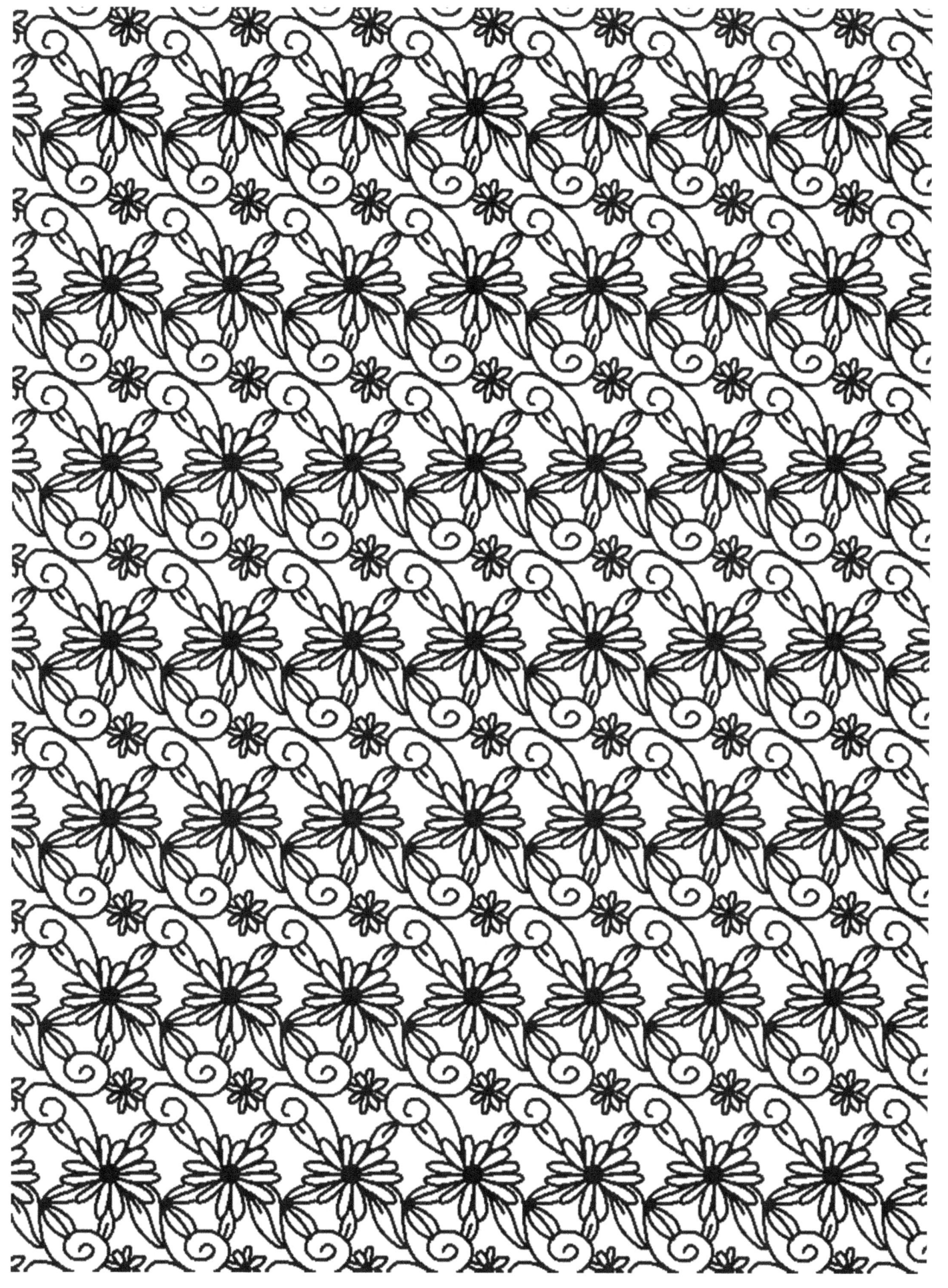

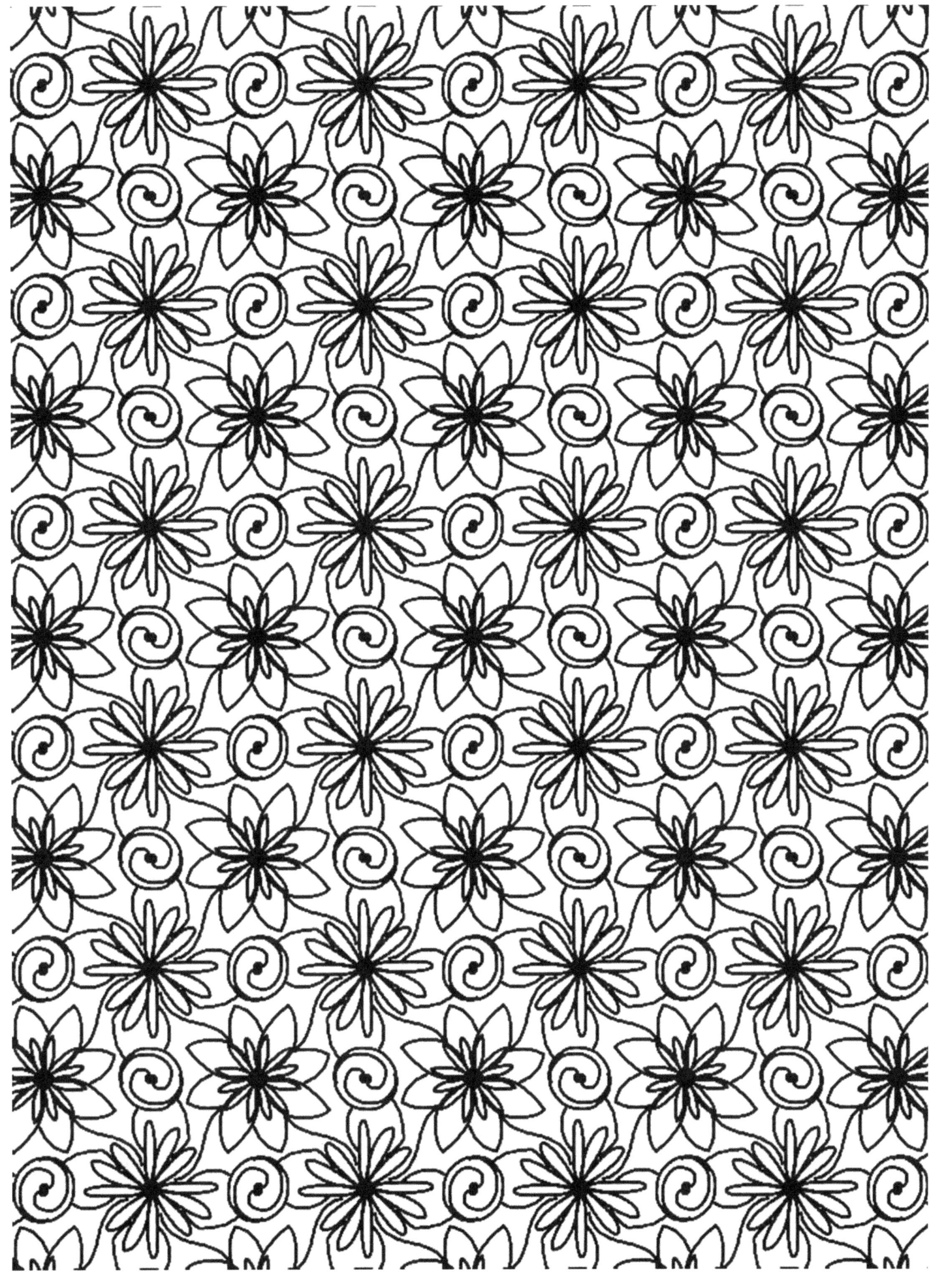

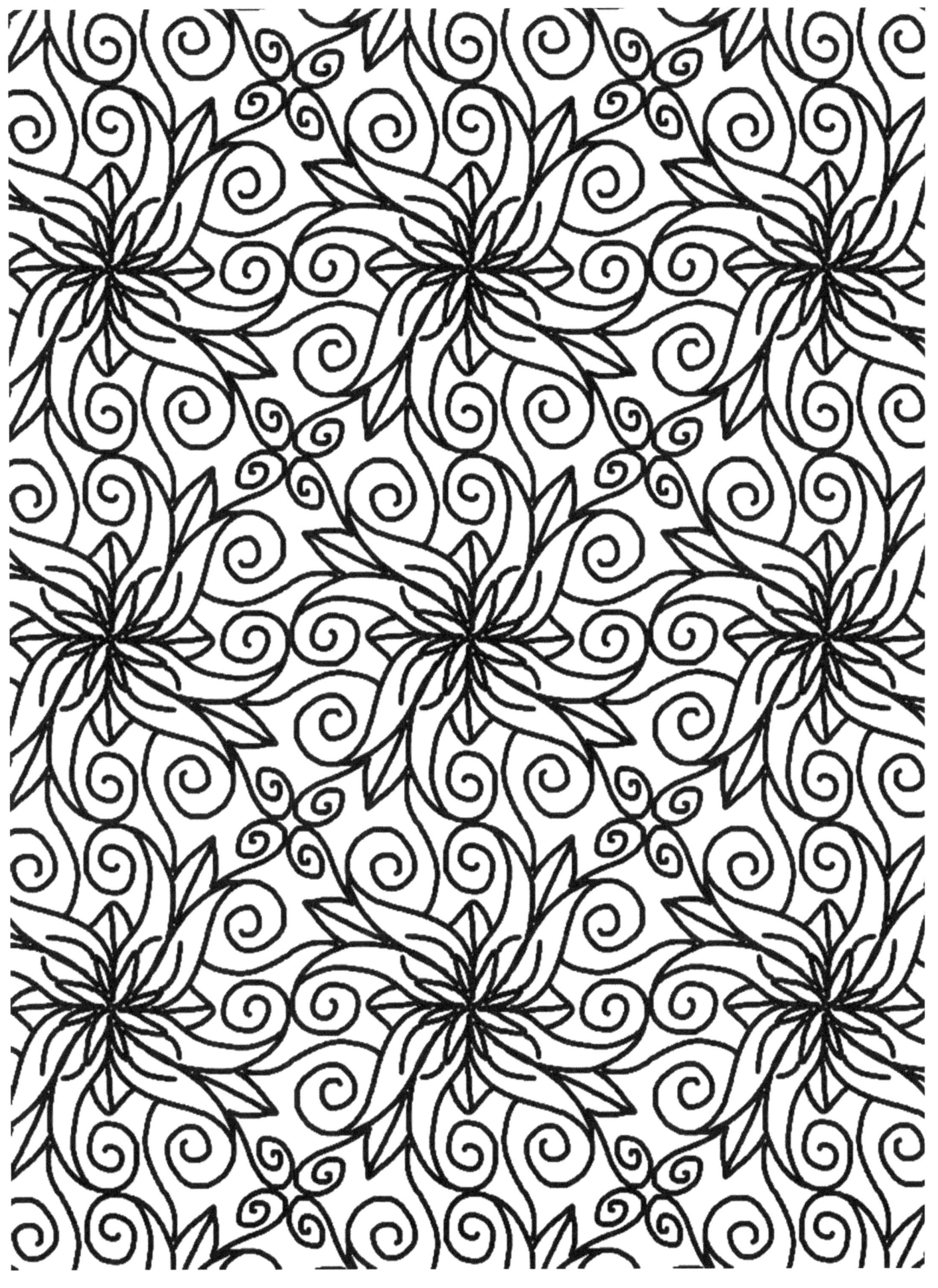

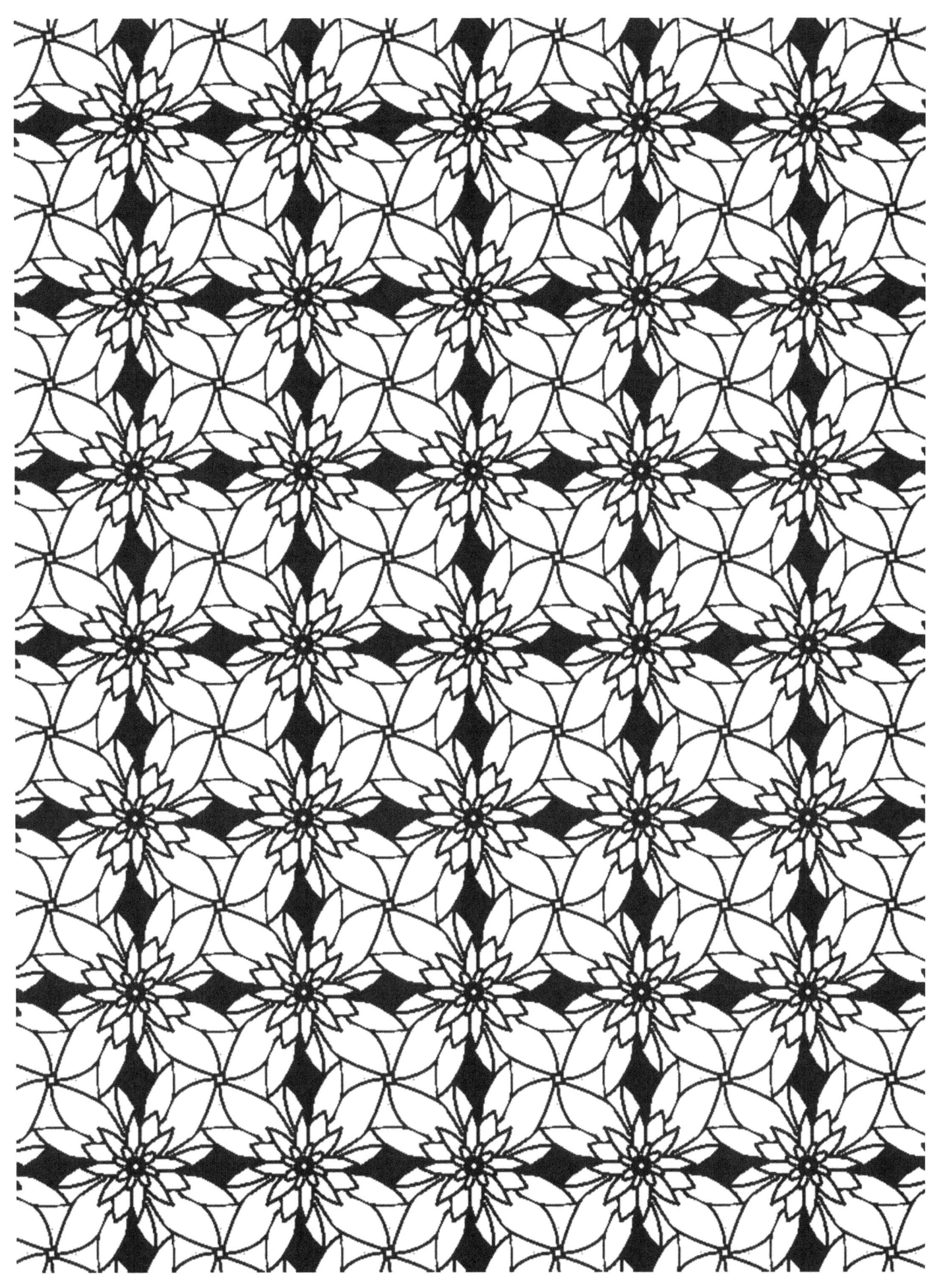

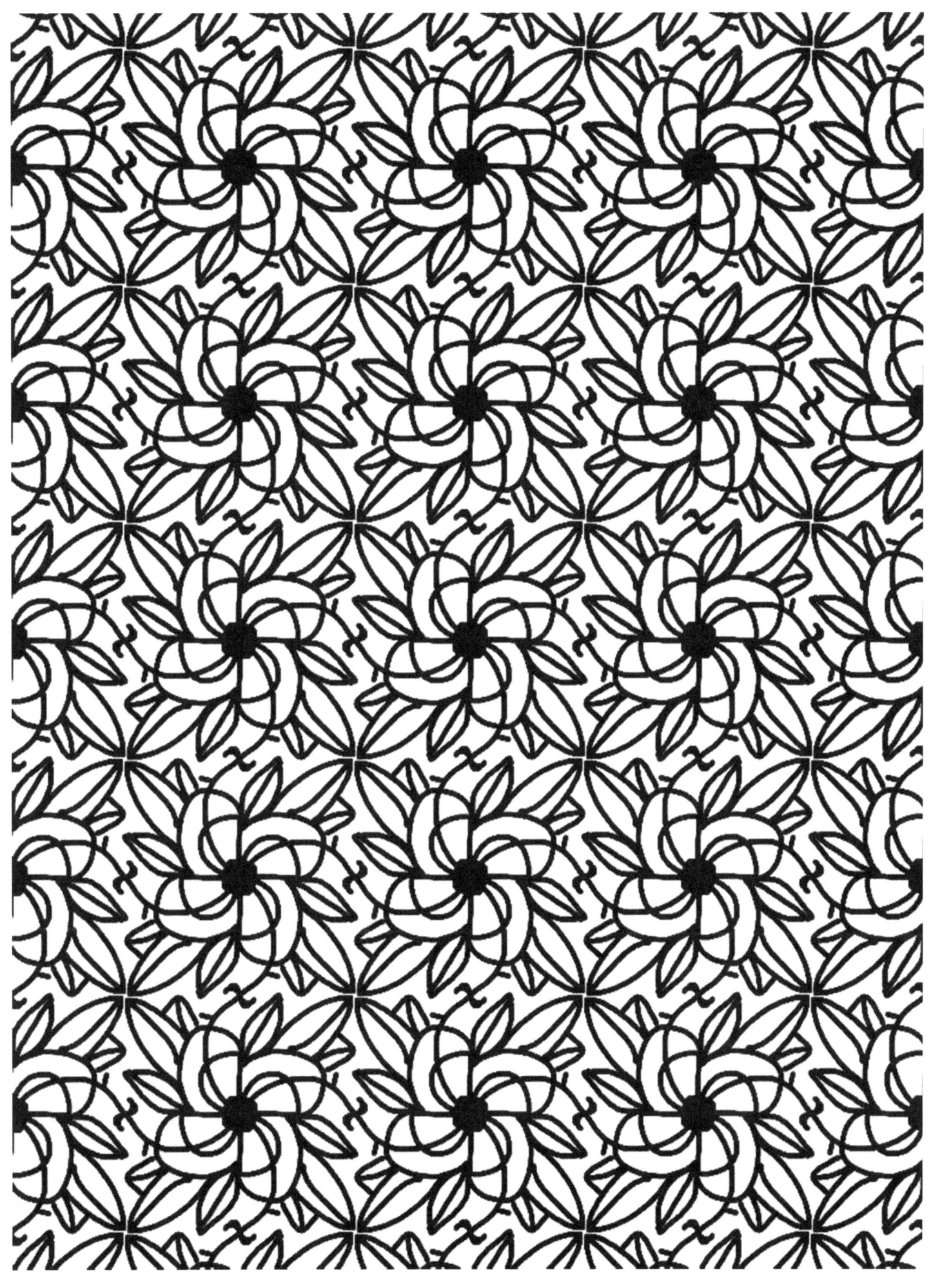

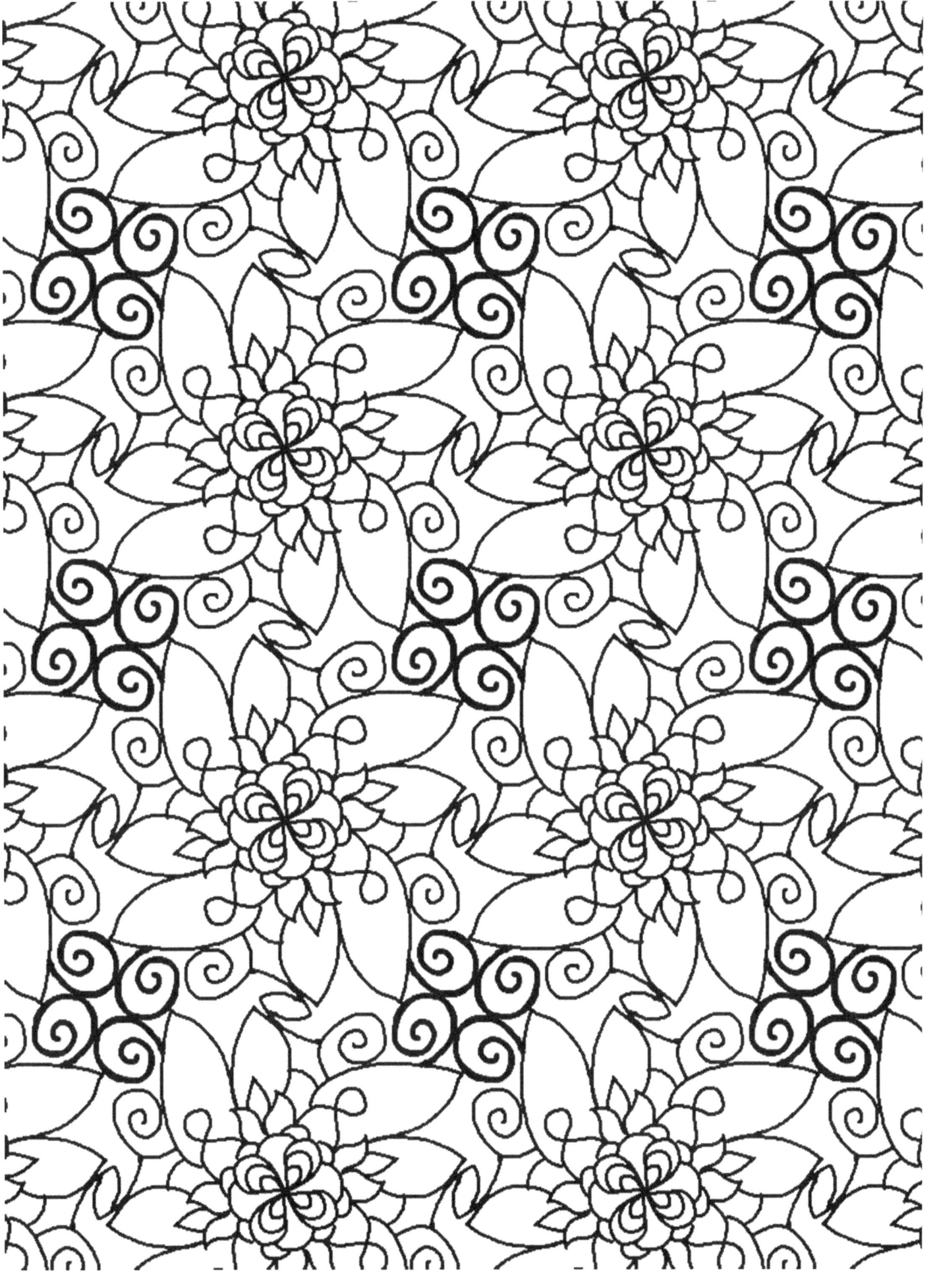